Making a Killing: The Scourge of the Global Arms Trade

SAGHIR IQBAL

ISBN-10: 1721773150
ISBN-13: 978-1721773152

DEDICATION

I dedicate this book to all those who gave me encouragement, support and guidance. Foremost, to my father (late) Raja Mohammed Iqbal and to my mother Azra Begum, from whom I have learnt so much. In addition to my wife Neghat Khan, who was patient and extremely helpful in my trying times. And finally I dedicate this to Raja Jahangir Khan, Raja Mohammed Yasin (Diamond), Raja Nadir Yasin and Raja Mohammed Naheem Khan.

CONTENTS

ACKNOWLEDGMENTS

I am very grateful to a host of people for their various contributions towards this book. I am particularly very grateful to Professor Syed Peerzada Mahmud Shah Bookhari who deserves much commendation for his constant encouragement and support throughout the hard times of the programme. In addition, I am also very grateful to Noreen Shah, Noreen Akhtar, Shaheen Hussain and Husnaa Tahir for their constant support.

SAGHIR IQBAL

Making a Killing: The Scourge of the Global Arms Trade

Various military equipment

Abstract

This books looks at the scourge of the global arms trade. Many countries and their respective Military-Industrial Complex (MIC) are 'making a killing' in the world's largest trade in the buying and selling of weapons. The MIC is an informal alliance between a country's military and the arms industry which supplies it, seen together as a vested interest which influences public policy. The arms trade is essentially the buying and selling of military technology – the equipment and skills required by a country to defend itself. The trade involves the transfer of resources, ranging from the materials used to build a weapon (e.g. –Steel and Aluminium) to the knowledge and information that is necessary to make it work.

Many countries are anxious to sell as many weapons as they can. The main political benefit that exporting nations hope to gain from selling arms is the extension of their influence to other countries and regimes. Since the end of the Second World War it has been common for countries to sell weapons, or even give them away, to make other countries friendly towards them. Major weapons (aircraft, missiles, tanks and ships) probably account for about one-half of the total trade in weapons and equipment. The remaining items traded include spare parts, small arms, ammunition and support equipment.

Tornado Strike combat aircraft armed with missiles and bombs

Abbreviation

AAM – Air-to-air missile

AAR - Air to air refuelling

A2/AD – Anti-access/Area-denial

APC – Armoured Personnel Carrier

ALCM/GLCM – Air Launched Cruise Missile/ Ground Launched Cruise Missile

AWACS – Airborne Warning and Control System

BVR – Beyond Visual Range (air-air-missile)

MBT – Main Battle Tank

MIC – Military-Industrial Complex

PGM - Precision guided munitions (Smart weapons)

SAM – Surface to Air Missile

UAV – Unmanned Aerial Vehicle
UCAV – Unmanned Combat Aerial Vehicle

USMC – United States Marine Corps

UN – United Nations

Rafale multi-role combat aircraft

1 MAKING A KILLING

Wheeled APC

Each year billions of dollars are spent on the arms trade between nations across the world, all the while millions of people continue to live in dire states in unimaginable poverty. Many will lose their lives and die due to hunger and hunger related diseases. Due to the current political and economic climate of society, increasing firepower is on the rise, countries are purchasing arms to showcase their strength as a nation which in turn means we must expect wars in the world to become heavily violent and destructive. Stavrianakis (2010) notes, "Military production and trade are dominated by the US, Russia and Western European states". He further mentions, "that the international trade is predominantly a North-South phenomenon: approximately two-thirds of all international arms transfers are to developing states" (Grimmett 2008).

Arms trade – what is it?

Buying and selling of military technology is referred to as the arms trade. This means the equipment and skill a country possesses in order to defend itself form external forces. The exchange of goods consists of a transfer of resources. These range from materials used to actually construct a weapon such as steel or aluminium to the knowledge and information that is necessary to make it work.

A sharp increase in the military budget across the world has continued despite the negative impact of the global financial crisis. Many countries have procured sophisticated 'State of the Art' weapons, with an emphasis of key 'game changing' items in the region – modern submarines, ships, aircraft and long range anti-ship missiles. For instance, the following purchases have been made:

- China has purchased Su35 Multi-role combat aircraft
- UK has purchased the F-35 Lightening II multi-role combat aircraft
- Vietnam is in the process of acquiring Russian Kilo class submarines
- Malaysia is obtaining F18 combat aircraft
- Japan has ordered the F35 Stealth Joint Strike Fighters
- South Korea has purchased the Apache Gunship helicopters
- Australia's purchase of 12 submarines, 100 F-35 Joint Strike Fighters and eight new warships
- India has purchased the French Rafael Combat aircraft
- Iraq has purchased US F-16 Fighting Falcon Fighter Jets

Many regions across the globe are sliding into an arms race due to the simmering differences amongst themselves. One countries purchase of weapons has given the impetus for a rival to obtain further arms. This increase in regional insecurity has resulted in the increase in military expenditure.

The arms trade has encouraged many countries to purchase weapons, which has ensured continued hostility amongst nations and also helps to prolong conflicts to devastating levels. Money spent on the arms trade has meant that essential services receive less income in their countries (health services, education, poverty reduction, deficiencies in welfare services etc.).

A brief look at some of the items purchased – the buying and selling of military technology and services.

Force Multipliers – 'Sophisticated Weapons'.

US Naval force projection firepower

Technology

Technological innovations in military technology have had a profound effect on strategy and the ability to have an edge in any conflict. Technology has given better situational awareness and long range precision strikes. State of the art offensive and defensive weapons have given the impetus for a new range of strategies and tactics.

Image/pixabay.com/anti-tank guided missile/T72 main battle tank

Images/pixabay.com/ v-22-osprey-boeing-helicopter/amphibian assault battalion convoy

Images/pixabay.com/USMC amphibious training/CH-53 Super stallion helicopter

Images/pixabay.com/F-15 Eagle combat aircraft/soldier training

Images/pixabay.com/army rangers parachuting/Hawkeye radar-aircraft-squadron

Network-Centric Warfare

Images/pixabay.com/monitor binary system/radar protection/US navy radar technicians/satellite communications

Network-centric warfare is a combination of factors that have enabled states to gain information on their adversaries. Network-centric seeks to gain an information advantage by the use of sophisticated information technology, into a competitive advantages through the use of computer networking of geographically dispersed forces. It allows all parties at different levels to be well informed. This level of coordination and information could be detrimental to any force.

In addition to this, the important emerging field of Information and Cyberwarfare that involves the battlespace use of computers and networks in warfare (tactical information, cyberattacks, espionage and sabotage). The importance of the use of an ever changing Battlespace can be essential in unifying military strategy to integrate and combine armed forces for the military theatre of operations (including air, information, land, sea, cyber and space to achieve military goals). The countries around the world are developing or improving these vital technologies.

Tankers

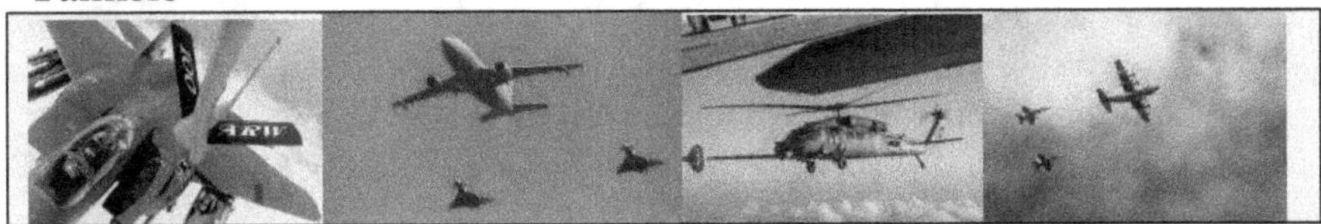

Images/pixabay.com/air to air refuelling/tankers/helicopter refuelling/Hercules tanker refuelling

Air to air refuelling by tankers have resulted an increase in the rage of combat aircraft. It has also allowed Combat patrol aircraft to extend its range and hence stay on patrol without having to land and refuel. The tankers have increased the range and loitering time within or near the designated target areas. It also allows fighter and bomber aircraft to carry extra weapons/bombs instead of extra fuel tanks.

Tankers are considered force multiplier aircraft as they allow fighter, bombers, special mission aircraft, transport aircraft to be rapidly deploy to the areas where they are needed.

Bombers

Images/pixabay.com/B1b bomber/B2 Spirit/F-15 Eagles and B1b bomber in South Korea

Bombers with precision guided bombs and missiles have been able to attack targets without the support of other aircraft such as, the need for large escort fighter aircraft, electronic warfare aircraft etc. Precision guided munitions (PGM) have given an attacking force the ability to strike with pin-point accuracy.

AWACS/Special Mission Aircraft

Images/pixabay.com/E3 Sentry/Self-defence/maritime aircraft

Fighter aircraft have been given significant support from an AWACS platform. Fighters can now approach targets without being revealed by their own radar. They can defend and strike key areas with higher confidence. Enemy aircraft or air defence systems can be picked up earlier by the AWACS aircraft and the information is given to the fighter aircrafts a lot earlier, thereby minimising the risks to the fighter aircraft.

Stealth

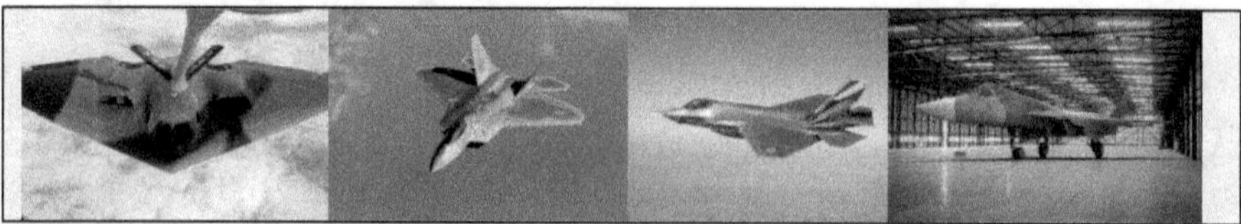

Images/pixabay.com/B2 Stealth bomber/F22 Stealth fighter/F-35 Stealth fighter/Russian T50 Pakfa stealth aircraft

Stealth technologies have given certain countries the ability to force multiply their military power. Stealth aircraft have a special design that reduces its chance of being detected by an adversary forces. It allows countries to undertake very dangerous missions in which a highly protected area can be taken out with military precision and the chance of the aircraft surviving is high. These technologies can be seen as game changing weapons that can cause substantial losses to an adversary with minimum losses to the launching nation. The Wars in Iraq and Bosnia had indicated the lethality of stealth.

UCAV/UAV

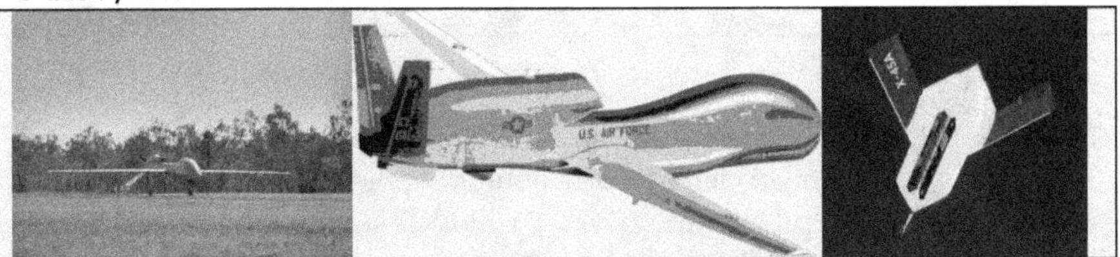

Images/pixabay.com/MQ-1c Predator drone/Global Hawk UAV drone/boeing-x-45a-aircraft-drone

Drones have become sophisticated and can be used for a number of operations, such as surveillance, gathering intelligence and patrolling airspace/borders/maritime reconnaissance etc. The unmanned combat aerial vehicle (UCAV) also known as combat drones, usually carry smart munitions and missiles to strike at designated targets. The drones are under real-time human control with different levels of autonomy. They are cheaper and safer to operate than manned combat aircraft.

Missiles

Images/pixabay.com/air to air missiles/laser guided bombs/ballistic missiles

Advances in sophisticated missiles ensures that the offensive and defensive use of them can alter the battlefield. Countries are developing and purchasing weapons that have long range strike abilities. Countries can now attack their adversaries at much longer and safer distances. Missiles come in different sizes and shapes and adapted for different purposes: surface-to-surface and air-to-surface missiles (ballistic, cruise, anti-ship, anti-tank, etc.), surface-to-air missiles (and anti-ballistic), air-to-air missiles, beyond visual range (BVR) and anti satellite weapons. These missiles have altered the scenes of a modern conflict and have given nations a number of choices in their use (stand-off capabilities).

Submarines

Images/pixabay.com/submarines

Submarines are hunters that operate in the oceans and have a number of roles to fulfil. The main defence of a submarine lies in its ability to remain concealed in the depths of the ocean. A hidden submarine is a real threat, and because of its stealth, can force an enemy navy to waste resources searching large areas of ocean and protecting ships against attack. Submarines operate in different roles, such as anti-shipping and mine-laying. The development of submarine-launched ballistic missile (SLBM) and submarine-launched cruise missiles (SLCM) gave submarines a considerable and long-ranged capability to attack both land and sea targets with a selection of weapons ranging from torpedoes, anti-ship, cluster bombs to nuclear weapons. Its purpose to achieve sea-denial for an adversary and to make it costly for an opponent country to attack (deterrence). It is also used for softening enemy targets at the incept of hostilities, as indicated in the Iraq, Bosnia, Afghanistan conflict – US navy Tomahawk long range missiles were used to attack key targets (Command & Control facilities, air defences, radar sites etc.).

Aircraft Carriers

Images/pixabay.com/aircraft carriers/F-18 Super Hornets landing and taking off on carriers

Aircraft carriers are true force multipliers and are a symbol of power projection capabilities of a nation. They are equipped with combat aircraft and helicopters and essentially a floating airbase. It allows countries to send their task force to a designated area and use it for air power deployment. It reduces the times and transit distances of aircraft and therefore significantly increase the time of availability on the combat zone. The Aircraft carriers have been used in a devastatingly manner in modern warfare. The aircraft carrier allows a naval force to project air power worldwide without depending on local bases for staging aircraft operations (they usually carry numerous sophisticated fighter planes, strike aircraft, helicopters, airborne early warning aircraft and other types of aircraft).

Arms Trade – trading in 'Death'

A number of force multiplier items are in either development or in the process of purchasing from other countries. These sophisticated weapons will enable adversaries to inflict serious damage to their respective targets. The increased income (GDP) has given the rivals an impetus to purchase these technologies. Hence any future conflict will have devastating effects in the region.

Typoon multi-role combat aircraft

The arms trade internationally has increased vastly since World War 2. Weapons such as aircraft, missiles, tanks and ships all account for about one-half of the total trade in weapons and equipment. Other items such as spare parts, small arms, ammunition and technical support equipment account for the remaining items. The arms trade internationally has become big business, it has been estimated to have reached $1739 billion in 2017, the highest level since the end of the cold war (SIPRI Year Book 2018).

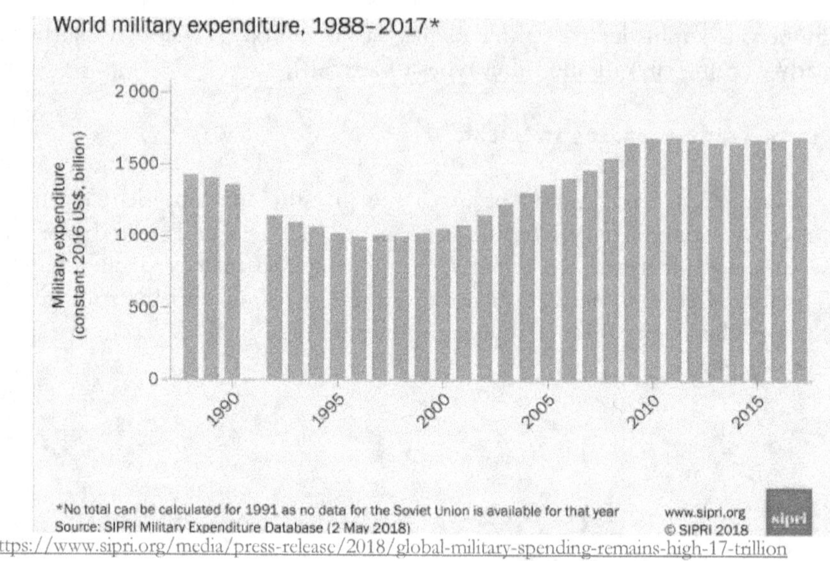

https://www.sipri.org/media/press-release/2018/global-military-spending-remains-high-17-trillion

Main Battle Tank (MBT) in the desert

The USA and the Soviet Union were perceived as super powers in 1945. Due to the war many countries of Europe had been restricted, more so weakened in regards to their economic and political strength. This led to the super powers to gain in strength and stature. The two super powers had various differences which surfaced just after the war and relations between the two were severed resulting in a cold war. Neither side was willing to declare war but both were prepared to do whatever it took to destabilise the other (Freedman, 1985).

APC in action

Combat helicopters

Over a period of time competition between the superpowers filtered into the developing world. These countries starting supplying weapons to the developing countries due to the competition for power and influence. It is thought they did this to further their own interests to supply arms to build rapport. The arms trade initial aim is to gain allies which with then in turn reduce the influence of rival power. For example, the USA had supplied arms to anti-communist governments such as South Korea, Pakistan and Israel. The USSR had supplied arms to movements trying to overthrow western style capitalist governments, and to anti-American countries such as Cuba or Libya. The arms trade helps each side in the 'cold war' obtain military facilities such as airports, military bases and harbours (Freedman, 1985).

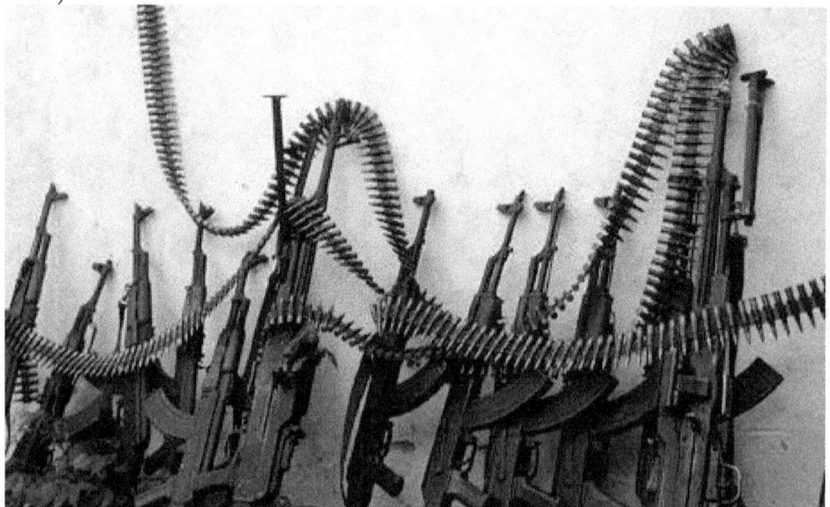

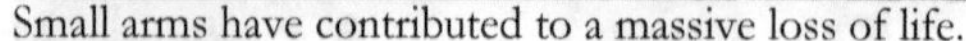

Small arms have contributed to a massive loss of life.

Young soldiers

2 WHY SELL ARMS?

Different nations have different reasons as to why they sell arms, and sometimes their justification can alter. The reasons given for selling arms can be categorised two fold, one being political/national security and second being economic reasons.

Some countries are very eager to sell as many weapons as they can. One of the political benefits a nation can hope to gain from selling arms to other allies is to extend their influence over other countries and their regimes. Since the end of the Second World War it has been common for countries to sell weapons, or even give them away, to make other countries friendly towards them (Freedman, 1985).

During times of war an exporting nation will see an opportunity to supply weapons to the side it believes will win. This is because that nation may be an ally of the exporter or alternatively it could be that it is an enemy of the exporter of arms. There are numerous reasons as to why a country may export and sell arms. The USA supplies weapons to the 'contra forces' fighting the Nicaraguan Government in Central America because it wants to see a change of government in that country. The Soviet Union supplies weapons to the governments of countries like Nicaragua, Angola and Ethiopia which were engaged in wars or conflicts because it wants them to survive (Freedman, 1985).

Another justification for selling arms to other countries is that it may help and create job prospects. The more that are sold whether that is in the home nation or abroad the more people are needed to develop and construct arms. Also it is widely believed that exporting weapons creates a good climate for further trade (Freedman, 1985).

In the early 1970's the arms trade had improved considerably, it was labelled as one of the fastest growing businesses in the world. One of the main reasons as to why there was a huge shift in arms trade was the new wealth of the oil producing countries especially in the middle east, this means that they had more money to spend on weapons (Freedman, 1985).

At the same time, the key players in exporting arms saw sales as a means of getting a return on large sums of money, which they were having to spend on oil and other commodities. It can be stated that war and crisis in every region of the world stimulated the trade further. The above factors allowed countries to ease their controls on trade (Freedman, 1985).

The World arms market in terms of sales is currently dominated by the West (Burrows, 2002). More than half of all major weapons were from USA, Russian and France- each state had accounted for more than 10 percent. Britain and Germany had accounted between five and ten percent. In addition, 15 percent of the World total arms sales were accounted by the next seven biggest sellers – Belarus, China, Ukraine, Italy, Israel and Spain (Burrows, 2002).

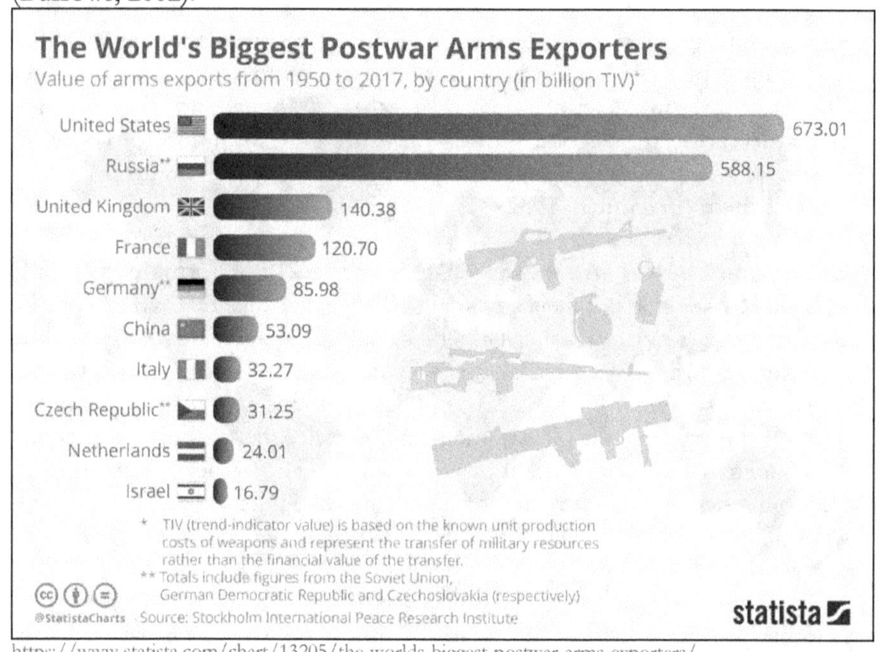

https://www.statista.com/chart/13205/the-worlds-biggest-postwar-arms-exporters/

The world arms market in terms of sales is led by the West. Between 1950 and 2017 the USA has been the largest exporter, selling up to a staggering $673.01 billion worth of sales. Russia was the next highest seller, exporting $588.15 billion worth of arms in the same period.

Between 1996 and 2000 over half of all major conventional weapons came from the USA, Russia and France – each had accounted for 10 percent. Britain and Germany had accounted between five and ten percent. In addition, 15 percent of the world total arms sales were accounted by the next seven biggest sellers – Belarus, China, Ukraine, Italy, Israel and Spain. (Adams,1992).

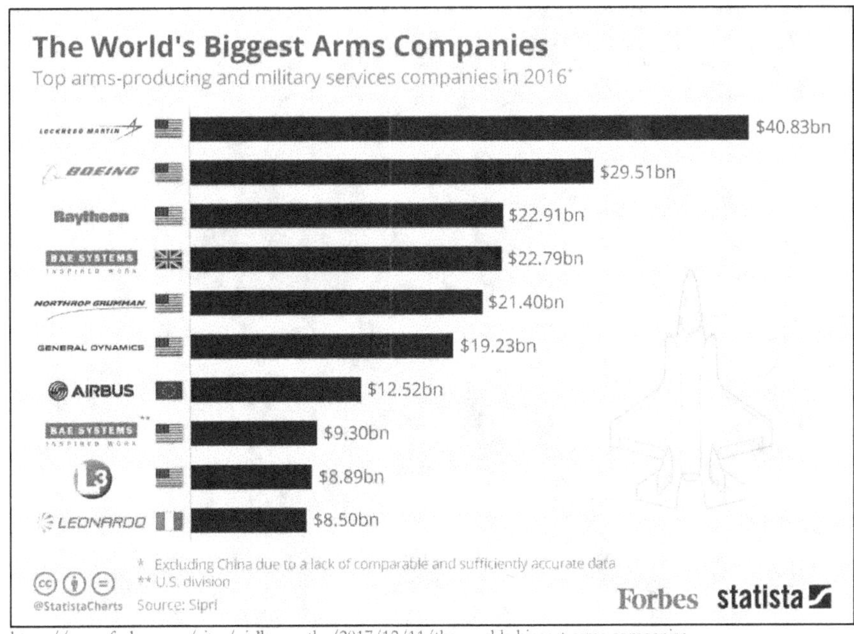

https://www.forbes.com/sites/niallmccarthy/2017/12/11/the-worlds-biggest-arms-companies-infographic/#19403715475a

The above graph shows the domination of the Military-Industrial Complex in the US.

Kilo Class Submarine

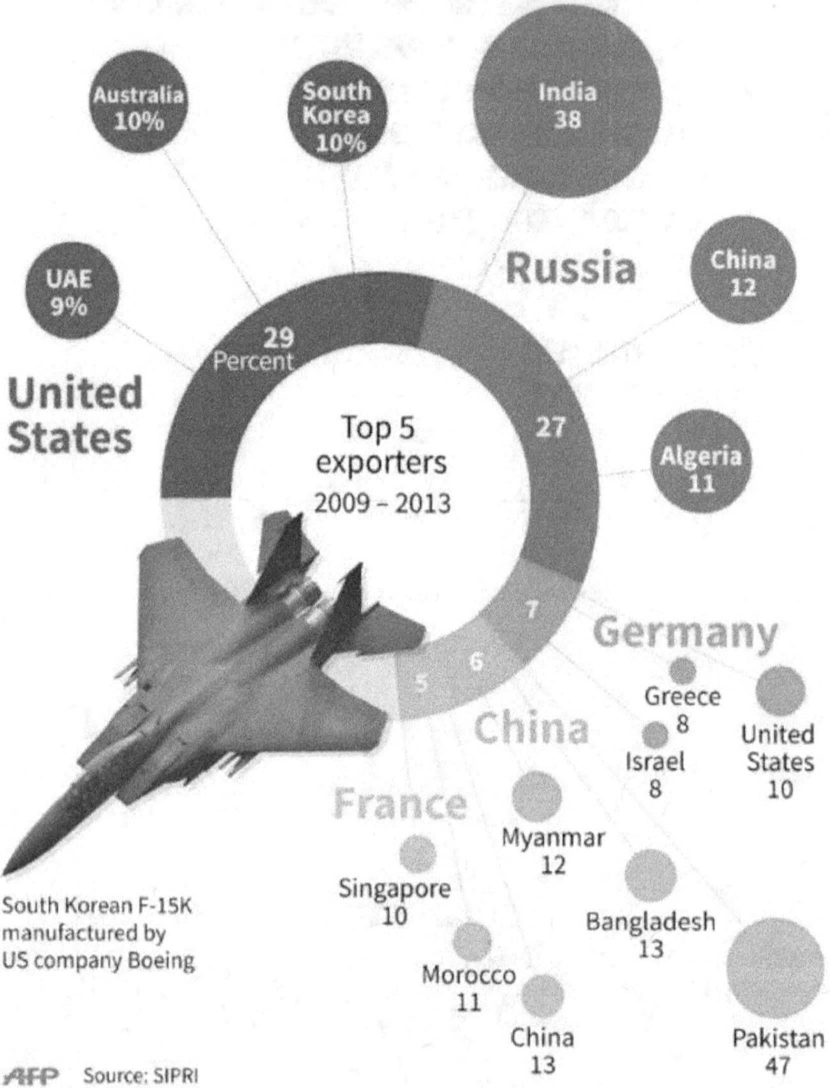

http://www.dailymail.co.uk/wires/afp/article-2884671/Global-arms-treaty-enters-force-Wednesday.html

The following is a list of some of the world's largest weapons manufacturers, sourced from data collated by the Stockholm International Peace Research Institute and published in 2016 (SIPRI).

Rank Company	**Country**	**Arms Sales**
Lockheed Martin	USA	Lockheed Martin sold $36bn of arms in 2015, turning a profit of $3.6bn that year, and as of October 2017 had a total market value of $91bn on the New York Stock Exchange
Boeing	USA	Known mostly for its line of passenger aircraft, Boeing made $28bn of arms sales in 2015, resulting in a profit of $5.2bn.
BAE Systems	UK	The UK's largest weapons manufacturer had arms sales of $26bn in 2015, which formed 93 percent of its total sales. BAE employs more than 82,000 people who help produce military equipment such as the Tornado warplane, Challenger tank, and drones for the British army and other states.
Raytheon	USA	In 2015, Raytheon turned over almost $22bn in arms sales and made just over $2bn in profit.
Northrop Grumman	USA	It made just over $20bn in 2015 and turned a profit of more than $2bn.
General Dynamics	USA	It turned over $19bn in arms sales in 2015.
Airbus Group	EU-wide	Like Boeing, Airbus is popularly known for its line of passenger aircraft that are in service among airlines across the globe. Arms sales make up 18 percent of its business or $12.9bn in sales.
United Technologies	USA	The company based in the state of Connecticut draws 16 percent of its sales from arms, which amounts to $9.6bn. Its most famous product is the Black Hawk helicopter used by the US military and others.
Leonardo/Finmeccanica	Italy	Formerly known as Finmeccanica,

(Italy)		Leonardo produces aircraft components, weapons systems, helicopters and armoured vehicles. In 2015, its arms sales totalled $9.3bn, which resulted in $584m of profit.
L-3 Technologies	USA	Headquartered in New York, L-3 produces surveillance, communications and weapons control systems for military and civilian purposes. It had arms sales of $8.8bn in 2015 and made $282m in profit.

The top 10 largest arms companies, in terms of military sales.
https://www.aljazeera.com/news/2017/10/world-biggest-arms-companies-171007084157108.html

Chinese warships

3 WHY BUY ARMS?

It can be said that every nation has the right to be able to defend itself. However, security and defence are terms with no accurate meaning. The USA claims to be insecure yet it has many nuclear weapons and an enormous conventional (non-nuclear) defence capability   In this constant evolving society there is no such thing as complete security for a nation but this has not halted countries attempting to achieve their 'arms trade' goals.

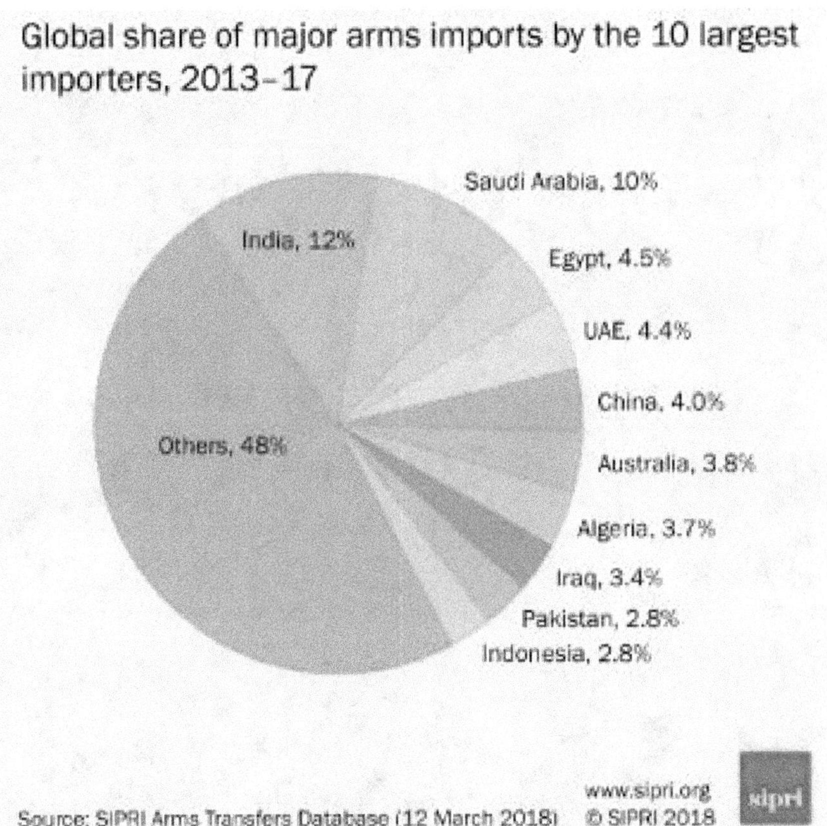

Many countries import arms for various reasons and most tend to relate to s nations problem of insecurity. The reason for this insecurity is firstly that a government has a right or rather a duty to protect their citizens and their own nations. Secondly the government has a duty to its citizens to protect their economy which includes raw material and industry.   Thirdly some countries purchase certain arms for the prestige attached.

In the developing world countries there are still a vast amount of territorial, political and religious disputes. Solving out these issues in the developing world countries can be a problem and this had led to conflicts and wars. For example, the Arab-Israeli conflict, Indo-Pakistan dispute over Kashmir. Ethnic disturbances and separatists claims resulting in violence and loss of life (e.g. Kurds in Turkey/Iraq/Iran have fought for a separate state). (Freedman, 1985).

In order to maintain these conflicts, countries had spent a large amount of their wealth in buying arms. This is what keeps the arms trade as lucrative market.

https://www.alaraby.co.uk/english/news/2016/10/27/new-un-peace-plan-for-yemen-leaves-out-hadi

Typhoon multi-role combat aircraft and US Warship

F-16 Fighting Falcon

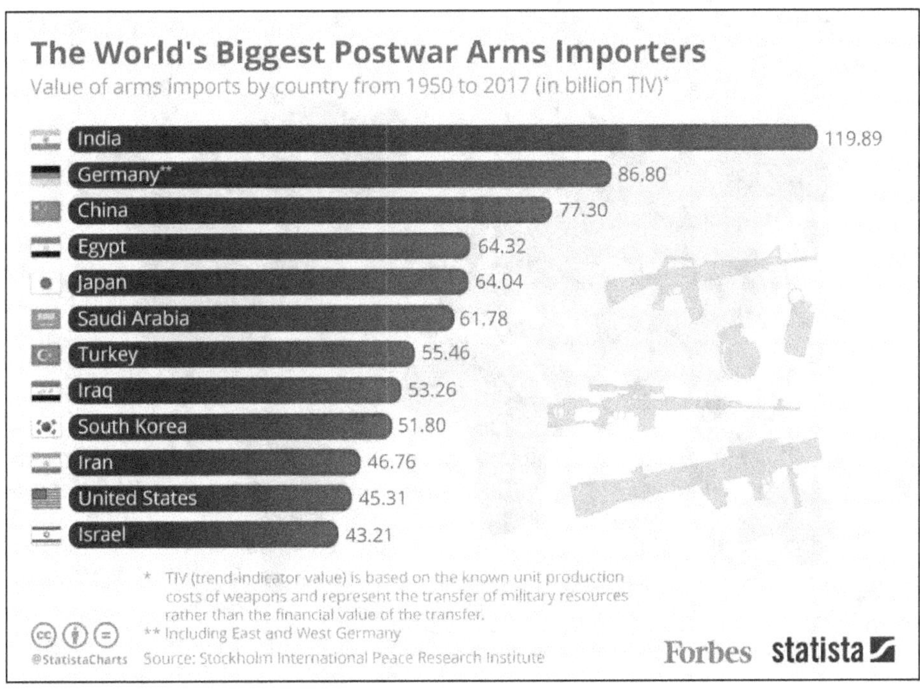

The World's Biggest Arms Importers Since 1950 -
https://www.forbes.com/sites/niallmccarthy/2018/03/12/the-worlds-biggest-post-war-arms-importers-infographic/#32e3fa118e34

Graphic shows examples of UK weapons used in Yemen's civil war.

https://www.graphicnews.com/en/pages/35249/YEMEN-UK-arms-used-in-conflict

SIPRI – Top 15 spending countries in 2017

Military spending by the top 15 spending countries in 2017, chart by SIPRI			Change, 2008–17 (%)	World share, 2017 (%)	Spending as a share of GDP (%)[b]	
Rank 2017	2016[a]	Country	Spending, 2017 ($ b.)			2017	2008
1	1	USA	610	–14	35	3.1	4.2
2	2	China	[228]	110	[13]	[1.9]	[1.9]
3	4	Saudi Arabia	[69.4]	34	[4.0]	[10]	7.4
4	3	Russia	66.3	36	3.8	4.3	3.3
5	6	India	63.9	45	3.7	2.5	2.6
6	5	France	57.8	5.1	3.3	2.3	2.3
7	7	UK	47.2	–15	2.7	1.8	2.3
8	8	Japan	45.4	4.4	2.6	0.9	0.9
9	9	Germany	44.3	8.8	2.5	1.2	1.3
10	10	South Korea	39.2	29	2.3	2.6	2.6
11	13	Brazil	29.3	21	1.7	1.4	1.4
12	11	Italy	29.2	–17	1.7	1.5	1.7
13	12	Australia	27.5	33	1.6	2.0	1.8
14	14	Canada	20.6	13	1.2	1.3	1.2
15	15	Turkey	18.2	46	1.0	2.2	2.2
Total top 15			1 396	..	80	..	..
World total			1 739	9.8	100	2.2	2.4

SIPRI – Top 15 spending countries in 2017 https://www.sipri.org/

Pakistan's Nasr Missile

India Enters Elite Club Of World's Five Biggest Spenders on Military

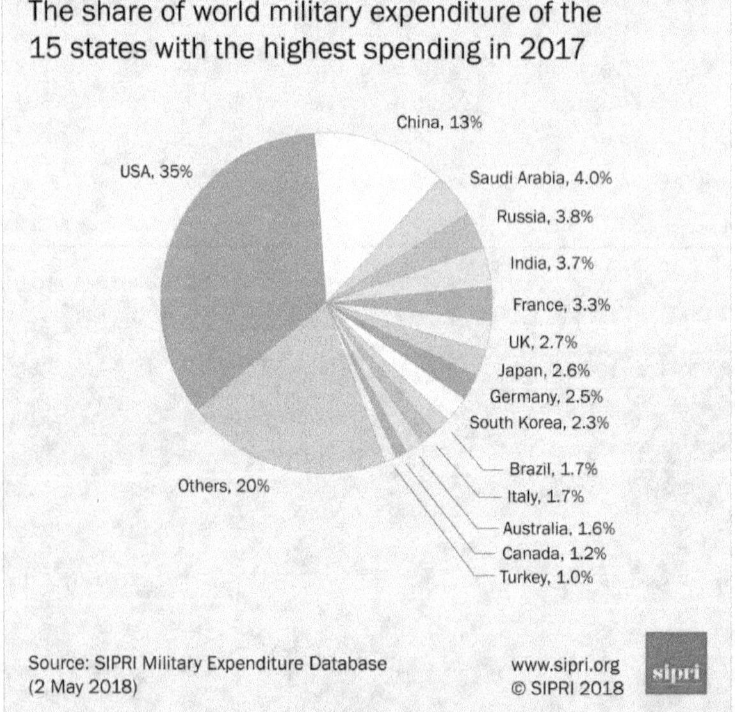

https://www.sipri.org/research/armament-and-disarmament/arms-transfers-and-military-spending/military-expenditure

According to the latest report by SIPRI, countries around the world spent $ 1.739 billion

Indian MBT

4 THE EFFECTS OF THE ARMS TRADE?

Researchers have predicted that over $1.739 trillion dollars are spent on military expenditure and arms worldwide. Thus, the arms trade has had a large effect on the world in different ways. This exchange of arms and war material increases the probability of conflict and can therefore be a threat to peace (SIPRI Year Book 2018). The transfer of important qualities of arms and war material had increased the possibilities of conflict and is therefore a threat to peace. In addition, the arms trade has sometimes prolonged and sustained wars, for example that of the Iran/Iraq conflict.

Surface to air missile system

The Iraq and Iran war in September 1980 lasted for 8 years. This war accumulated huge amount of money mainly due to the expenditure used in arms and man power. The war had over 500,000 casualties. To kill that many people, both sides had spent around $500,000 billion dollars, a substantial proportion of this on weapons, in what was the single largest bonanza for freelance arms dealers seen anywhere in the world at any time (Adams, 1992).

Iran-Iraq War: The Iraqi front.

In this case, the arms trade had maintained this war which would have ended a lot sooner. But instead it because so gruesome that it resulted in many deaths, destroyed the infrastructure and environment of the countries. The arms trade eventually led certain countries into very expensive arms race. It can be stated that the arms trade can reduce the chance of political conflicts being resolved peacefully and successfully.

Iran-Iraq War

The resulting arms competition increase political tension. In extreme circumstances, one of the nations may conclude that war is inevitable, that the balance of power is likely to worsen in the future, and that it should take pre-emptive military action to remove the threat poised against it. For example: that of Pakistan and India.

PAF US Made F-16 (block 52) multirole combat aircraft

PAF F-16B dual seat combat aircraft

Pakistan had purchased some expensive fighter aircraft (F-16s) from the USA in the early 1980s and therefore had qualitatively improved its air forces offensive capabilities. In return India bought advanced fighter aircraft from France (Mirage 2000s) and Russia (Mig-29s) in order to counter Pakistan. Also in other defence related areas, each side continued buying advanced and therefore very expensive systems. From tanks, ballistic missiles and eventually to nuclear weapons and despite this, still both countries were buying more firepower – the acquisition of further arms was actually undermining their security. It was really to all intents and purposes making them more insecure. The insecurity that had resulted could on the balance of probabilities lead to a potential war with terrible devastation for both countries. All of this was a result of the arms trade (Cordesman, 1988). All of this was a result of the arms trade.

IAF Su-30MKI multi-role combat aircraft releasing its bombs

Indian Air Force MiG-29 Strike Fighter

MIG-29 Fulcrum's armaments

Both of the above countries are very poor and experience many domestic problems. Poverty, child labour, homelessness are a few serious issues internally for both countries. The money they spend in arms could be utilised to improve the conditions of its people, and try and eradicate poverty and diseases, provide education and have adequate health facilities for its people.

Some countries have supplied arms in a bid to become friendly with other governments, so that it becomes hostile towards the supplier and therefore the weapons it sold being used against it. For example: that of the United Kingdom and Argentina. The Falklands war, showed that the weapons the UK had supplied were used against it, inflicting many casualties over it (Freedman, 1985).

The Type 42 destroyer HMS SHEFFIELD on fire after being struck by an AM.39 Exocet Missile.[1]

The arms trade has also proved that it can support and intensify conflicts due to different groups support for the war such as Vietnam War (supplied by America on the one side and Russia on the other side), the Arab/Israeli conflict, Gulf wars, and wars in Africa, South America and Asia (Freedman, 1985). Resulting with millions of death and vast damage to the environment, destruction of cities. Causing poverty, hunger, hunger related diseases, refugees etc.

---

[1] Imperial War Museum - https://www.iwm.org.uk/history/a-short-history-of-the-falklands-war

Israeli US F-16 combat aircraft

https://www.palestinecampaign.org/events/newcastle-psc-rally/

It can be stated that the arms trade has affected governments in that it has stimulated and indirectly persuading them to spend more money on buying arms, rather than spending that money to improve the quality of life of its people (Freedman, 1985).

The arms trade is such that it has become a mechanism to spend more money to defend citizens against a possible attack, rather than spending money against everyday ravages of poverty, life threatening diseases, and social issues such as employment in many countries.

The arms trade diverts funds from addressing current needs but it has a long term effect on issues like productivity in civilian industries, price hikes, a slowing economy etc. It can be concluded that the arms trade has become a mechanism to divert vital funds from significant issues such as poverty and hunger. Hunger has a detrimental effect and many countries currently are facing huge problems. According to some sources (WHO) over **800 million individuals are chronically undernourished, and face a long and gruelling death**. Death related to hunger and starvation average 50,000 a day. In Africa alone, 5 million children died from hunger-related causes.

Key numbers

Hunger and food security
- According to WHO, the overall number of hungry people in the world: 815 million, including:
  - In Asia: 520 million
  - In Africa: 243 million
  - In Latin America and the Caribbean: 42 million
- Share of the global population who are hungry: 11%
  - Asia: 11.7%
  - Africa: 20% (in eastern Africa, 33.9%)
  - Latin America and the Caribbean: 6.6% (World Health Organization, 2017).

http://www.who.int/news-room/detail/15-09-2017-world-hunger-again-on-the-rise-driven-by-conflict-and-climate-change-new-un-report-says

Malnutrition in all its forms
- Number of children under 5 years of age who suffer from stunted growth (height too low for their age): 155 million
  - Number of those living in countries affected by varying levels of conflict: 122 million
- Children under 5 affected by wasting (weight too low given their height): 52 million
- Number of adults who are obese: 641 million (13% of all adults on the planet)
- Children under 5 who are overweight: 41 million
- Number of women of reproductive age affected by anaemia: 613 million (around 33% of the total)

The impact of conflict
- Number of the 815 million hungry people on the planet who live in countries affected by conflict: 489 million
- The prevalence of hunger in countries affected by conflict is 1.4 - 4.4 percentage points higher than in other countries
- People living in countries affected by protracted crises are nearly 2.5 times more likely to be undernourished than people elsewhere (World Health Organization, 2017).

http://www.who.int/news-room/detail/15-09-2017-world-hunger-again-on-the-rise-driven-by-conflict-and-climate-change-new-un-report-says

Thomason (2016) mentions, "the use of child soldiers in armed conflict is an increasing global concern" and further contends, "child soldiers often report feeling guilt for the wrongs they commit". Child soldiers are usually coerced into taking arms for their respective sides and are subject to many horrors of conflict. With their mind-set used to the trauma of conflict will find it difficult to set themselves in the future to a peaceful co-existence (as they have only know the barbarism of armed conflict).

"To kill the big rats, you have to kill the little rats."
This was broadcast by a Rwanda radio during the genocide in 1994, where some 300,000 children were said to be killed. (Cited from the UNICEF State of the World's Children 1996 report, section on Children in War)[2]

The UN had been trying to get the Security Council to openly condemn any military that uses children in any way for a conflict.

According to UNICEF[3]: Recent advances in warfare have considerably intensified the dangers for children. Throughout the

---

[2] Children, Conflicts and the Military - http://www.globalissues.org/article/82/children-conflicts-and-the-military

[3] UNICEF - https://www.unicef.org/

last decade, it is estimated that child victims have included:

2 million killed;
4-5 million disabled;
12 million left homeless;
more than 1 million orphaned or separated from their parents; some 10 million psychologically traumatized.

In addition, there are an estimated 120,000 child soldiers in Africa. This is nearly half the total of 300,000 around the world.[4]

Child soldiers

Hence peace education can be a positive mechanism for change in this ever increasing violent world. Peace education may be able to influence people to spend their national wealth on more worthy things rather that to the arms trade or aka the 'Death trade'.

[4] Ibid

Russian sophisticated fighter jets

US Soldiers on a military training exercise

5 THE GLOBAL SMALL ARMS MENACE

AKMs, H&K G3 and RPG-7s found by U.S. Marines in Fallujah

Small arms are so abundant in the arms trade and have caused considerable amount of devastation around the world, the trade in them is so difficult to control and the devastation caused by them is so severe. They are produced in their millions for the reason that they are small and relatively cheap to manufacture, easy to trade on, smuggle, hide, steal, seize from an enemy or buy over the counter.

Small Arms—they cause 90% of civilian casualties[5]

Accordingly, there are approximately half a billion military small arms around the world; between 300,000 – 500,000 people around the world are killed by them each year. The small arms are the major cause of civilian casualties in modern conflicts (Shah, 2006).

---

[5] http://www.globalissues.org/article/78/small-arms-they-cause-90-of-civilian-casualties

Small arms

The category for small arms includes all of the following military, police and domestic weapons: revolvers and self-loading pistols, assault rifles, sub-machine guns and light machine guns, heavy machine guns, hand-held under-barrel and mounted grenade launchers, portable anti-tank and anti-aircraft guns, recoilless rifles, portable launchers of anti-tank and antiaircraft systems, and mortars of less than 100 mm calibre.

They are used by police and security patrols, by national armies and by guerrilla and revolutionary group's, they are carried by civilians legally in a number of countries, for sport in many more, and illegally in every country. They feature in basically every armed conflict between nation-states, in internal and civil wars, as status symbols and in gang fighting. According to the Small Arms Survey, 'The total number and global distribution of small arms remains one of the greatest enigmas in the field of international peace and security'.

<u>Landmines (Part of small arms)</u>

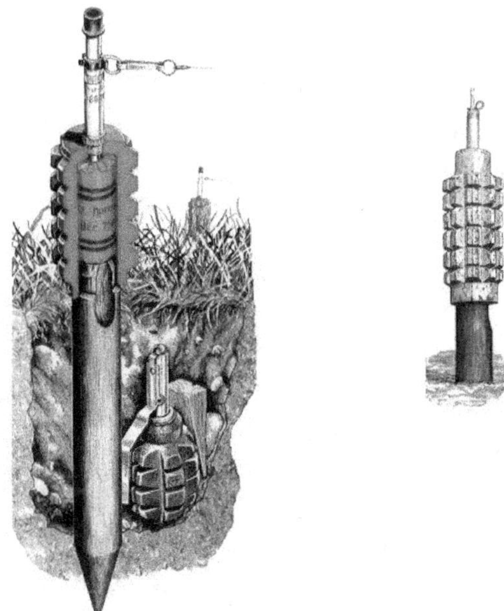

POMZ-2M mine with bubble trap system

Landmines are arguably the cruellest weapons sold by the arms dealers, with the biggest impact on civilians. Landmines cannot discriminate between the soldier and the civilian. Their impact cannot be confined to the duration of the battle; this has resulted in many civilian casualties.

Antipersonnel mines are one of the most harmful and indiscriminate instruments of war

Whether anti-tank or anti-personnel, the consequence of landmines on civilian communities is the same. They kill and injure indiscriminately, killing children just as easily as heads of households. Families are shattered by the loss of a loved one and also because their means of income or a future generation is destroyed. Those victims who are not killed when a landmine explodes are maimed or permanently disabled, thereby becoming a lasting financial and emotional burden on families. (24)

Landmines warning sign

Landmines also have devastating effects when they don't kill or maim, rendering thousands of acres of land unusable for farming or livestock. Families are usually forced to make a dreadful choice between starvation or risking their lives on mined fields.

There were 35,000 amputees as a result of landmines in Cambodia alone, and these were just the survivors. Overall, in the past few decades there have been over hundreds of thousands of deaths incurred as a result of Mine deaths and injuries. They are a daily threat in Angola, Bosnia, Afghanistan, Cambodia, Croatia, Chechnya, Lebanon, Iraq, Mozambique, Nicaragua, Somalia and numerous other countries.

CLUSTER BOMBS

Nearly 100 countries are signing a treaty to ban cluster bombs, while the leading producers of the bombs, including the US, Russia, China and Israel, remain outside the pact.

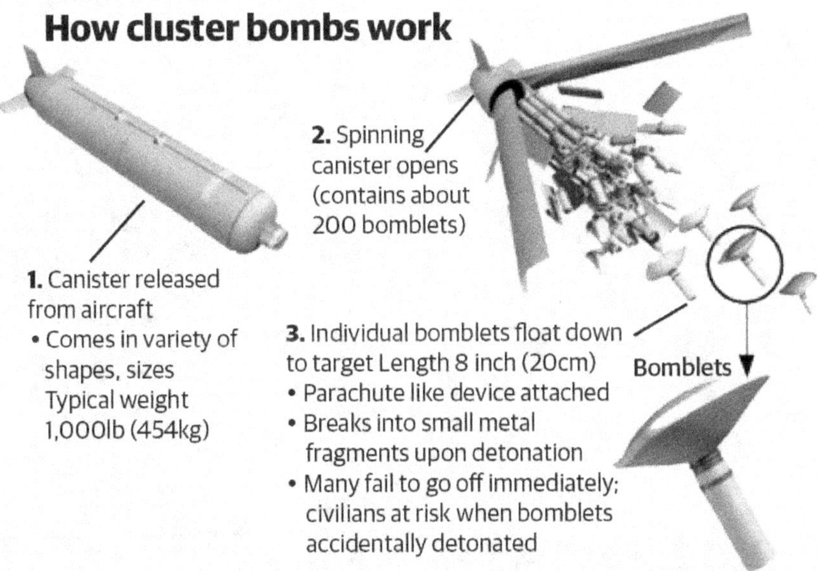

Since the 1960s, more than 20,000 cluster bombs casualties have been documented
https://www.dhakatribune.com/world/europe/2016/09/02/deadly-legacy-cluster-bombs

<u>Impact on human rights</u>

Human rights violations have not been a primary barrier to weapons sales at any time in history. The world's nastiest dictators, tyrants, human rights abusers and anti-democratic governments have been the customers of all of the major arms supplying countries in the world and still continue to be so. For instance, Israel is considered as one of the worst human rights abusing state across the Middle East region. There are ongoing tensions between Israel and its Palestinian population in the West Bank and Gaza part of the country. Since the formation of the Israeli State (on the former nation of Palestine), the Israeli government and its military has been at war against the Palestinian population, who are seeking to get their country back from Israeli occupation.

A two-state solution has been proposed to resolve this intractable long term conflict – however, the right wing government of Benjamin Netanyahu has no real intentions of resolving this and just wants to usurp the Palestinian land and eradicate Palestinian history and culture. With a strong Zionist lobby across the world (especially the USA) it continues to deliberately tell a false narrative of its intentions for a peaceful resolution with the Palestinian population. It has continued to promote the Palestinians in a negative light and has continued to tarnish its reputation.

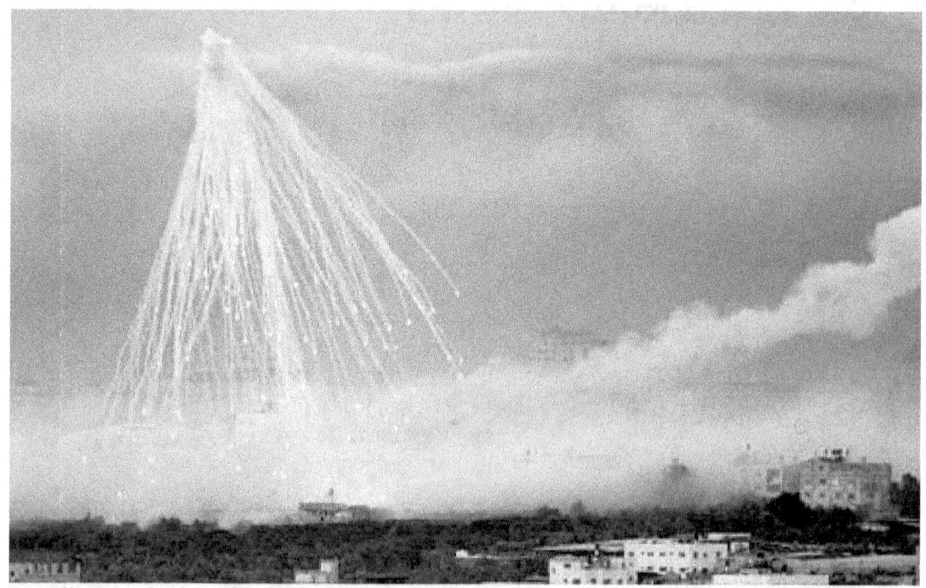

Israeli use of white phosphorus on the Palestinians has caused outrage and horrendous killings of the Palestinian population in Gaza. https://www.flickr.com/photos/free_world/3223064725

Palestinians being subjected to an Israeli Phosphorus attack

Israeli Prime Minister Benjamin Netanyahu and his hardline policy on the Palestinian population. According to Human Rights Watch (HRW), this nothing more that war crimes committed by the Israeli State (state terrorism at its best). HRW states, **"Israel's repeated firing of white phosphorus shells over densely populated areas of Gaza during its recent military**

campaign was indiscriminate and is evidence of war crimes".[6]

White Phosphorus Use Evidence of War Crimes

Indiscriminate Attacks Caused Needless Civilian Suffering

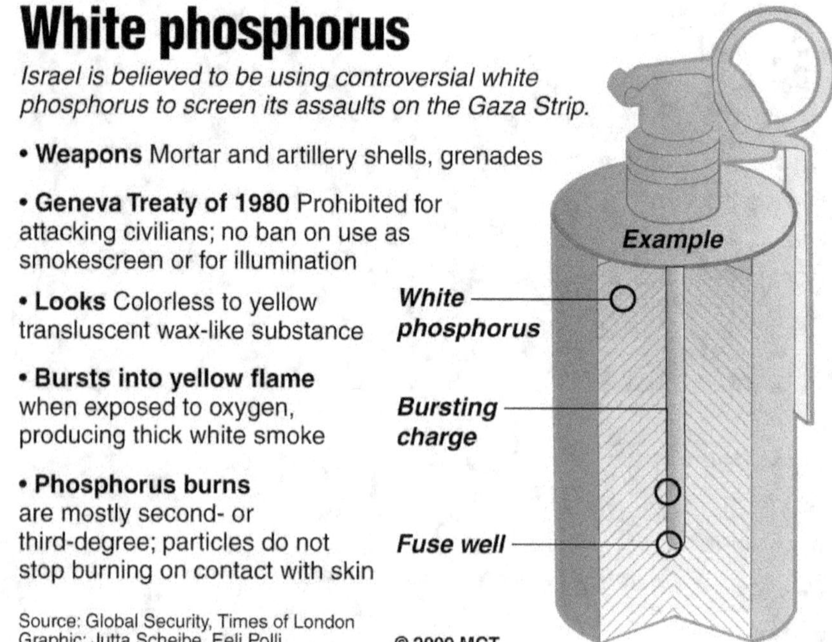

Some of the tactics undertaken by some Palestinians group have been ruthless on numerous occasions. They include bombings, kidnapping and extortion, but the Israeli response has been the systematic suppression of the Palestinian people. Since the outbreak of the conflict, many tens of thousands of Palestinian people have been killed, and millions have been displaced.

In May 2018 , the United Nations (UN), were outraged by continuous killing of Palestinian people by Israel. *'Enough is enough': UN condemns Israel as Palestinians bury their dead – video report[7]*. Israel

---

[6] Human Rights Watch (HRW) - https://www.hrw.org/news/2009/03/25/israel-white-phosphorus-use-evidence-war-crimes

[7] Guardian - https://www.theguardian.com/world/video/2018/may/15/enough-is-enough-un-condemns-israel-as-palestinians-bury-their-dead-video

has strong support from the Zionist lobbies across the globe and especially the USA and hence believes it is above the norms of international relations. There is widespread evidence to suggest that if the Israeli government does not resolve this conflict with the Palestinians then there could be a catastrophic conflict in the near future – this would not be in the interest of any as there will be further loss of lives. The cycle of conflict would cause further hatred and hence insecurity in the country and the region at large.

<u>Debt</u>

Arms sales fuel a never-ending cruel cycle of poverty and debt. The poorest countries in the world are so poor primarily because of massive debts owed to the developed world, much as repayments for previous arms sales. Many of the most heavily indebted countries are currently occupied in, or emerging from, conflict of some kind.

Greece's 1953 Write-off of Germany's War Debt[8]

As mentioned earlier, during the Cold War, developing nations found themselves filing in behind one or the other of the major world powers, buying or taking free arms to bolster their position. This in turn intensified local arms races. At the same time, dictators and corrupt governments were preparing large-scale arms purchases, both to boost their own power and to line their pockets with generous backhander's and bribes from each sale.

---

[8] https://www.globalresearch.ca/the-fragile-future-of-the-eu-greeces-1953-write-off-of-germanys-war-debt/5461652

High increases in military spending had significantly reduced the outlay on development and had contributed largely to the occurrence of cross-border and internal conflicts. This created a need for more arms, which were bought using predominantly Western loans, thereby adding to the country's debt.

Social impacts of Debt

An F-16 combat aircraft

The money spent on social and developmental programs in many countries has been reduced due to money being spent on servicing debts or money spent on further arms acquisition. Thus the servicing of debt for arms sales has affected health and education programs in numerous countries, contributing to other social impacts in the developing world.

Jobs

The arms trade is an immoral business that has caused numerous deaths and suffering of human beings around the world. Governments argue that selling arms to other countries helps to create employment. The more weapons that are sold at home or abroad, the more people are needed to develop and manufacture them. They further argue that these people are specifically trained in this vital and highly skilled area and would not be employable in any other field.

Defence Giant BAE Systems

Gun manufacturer

However, in reality it can be argued that selling arms is a business that does not really bring huge economic or employment benefits to the biggest arms-exporting countries. In many cases, high government subsidies, tax breaks, insurance schemes and promotion for arms manufacturers cost governments more money than weapons producers generate for them. Personnel employed in this field can easily be re-trained for another appropriate job – as is the case with numerous people who leave certain fields for another area.

Raytheon made $2bn in profit in 2015 [Kacper Pempel/Reuters]
https://www.aljazeera.com/news/2017/10/world-biggest-arms-companies-171007084157108.html

A Eurofighter Typhoon fighter jet on display at the Farnborough International Airshow, a biennial UK arms fair (https://www.caat.org.uk/issues/introduction)

Just six countries export 74% of the world's weapons!

https://claimyourinnocence.wordpress.com/2012/06/11/amnesty-international-usa-support-a-strong-arms-trade-treaty-this-july/

Mercenaries

Mercenaries can be seen primarily as purchasing people for certain operations (selling trained military manpower to be used in any given operation). Mercenaries come under a number of appearances, but all include the requirement of military might or instruction for a profit. Under the pretext of 'security' for example, private military companies, consultants, advisors or training outfits, all manner of services to both governments and companies are supplied, including full partaking in conflicts, the supply of arms, and armed defence/security of governmental officials (as in the case of Iraq), royal families and industrial machinery.

The ethics of a mercenary

Mercenary team

Rich and Poor gap

Moreover, the arms trade also effects the distribution of economic growth that does occur. It contributes significantly to the widening of the gap between the rich and poor countries, a focal point of increasing world tensions and anxiety. The poorest nations suffer from the deepening military competition between them.

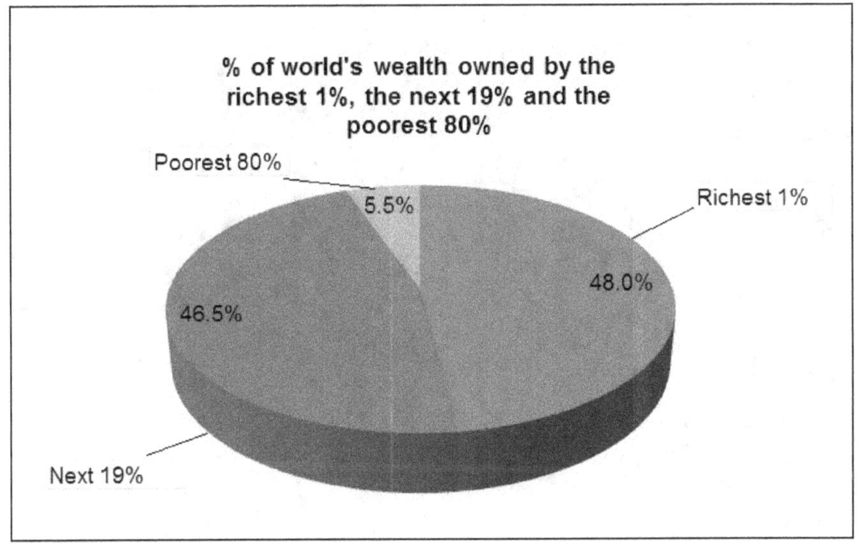

Source Oxfam

Oxfam calculated that the richest 1% of people in the world owned nearly half (48%) of the world's wealth. The vast majority of the remaining 52% of the world's wealth was owned by the next 19% of the world's richest people leaving just 5.5% of the world's wealth for the poorest 80% of people in the world.
(source - https://sustainingcommunity.wordpress.com/2015/01/21/even-it-up/)

Overall, the arms trade has affected the world in large, in many ways. It has caused more tensions between nations and has largely made them more insecure. It has diverted funds from necessary needs to buying weapons of destruction.

(Left) Inequality—the gap between the rich and the poor

result for poverty

Children-Poverty

Poverty

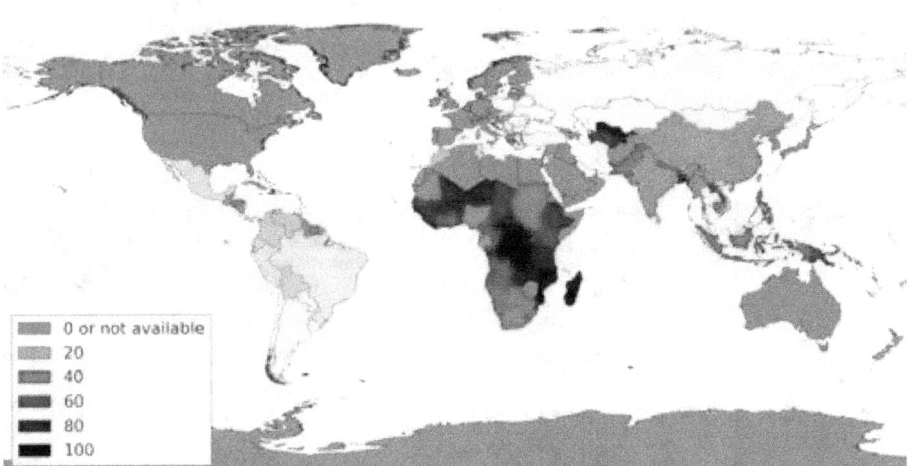

List of countries by percentage of population living in poverty

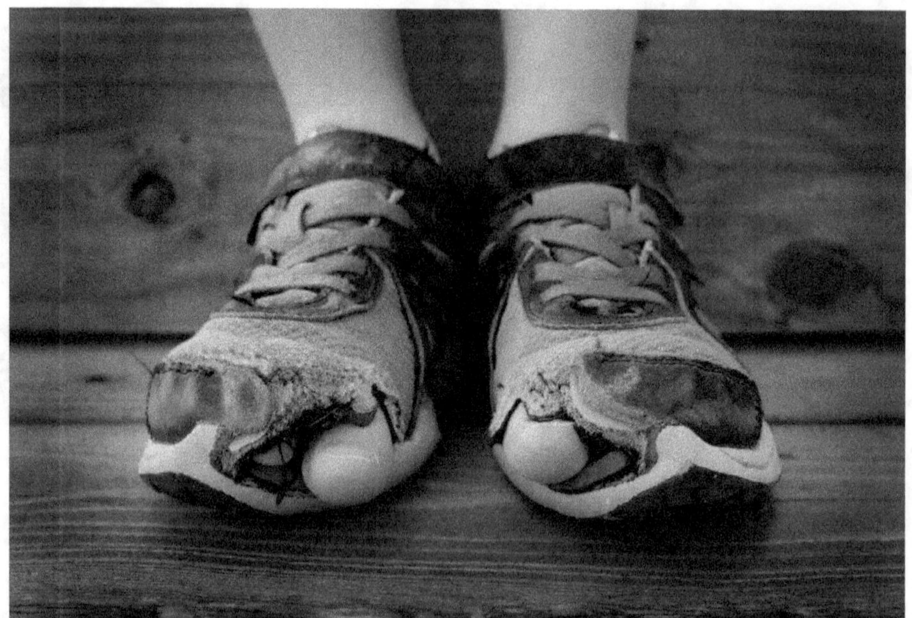

Poverty is a state of impoverishment, lack, or scarcity of certain resources that the individual or country needs to achieve and sustain good health, happiness, and well-being. (https://gibbshappinessindex.com/articles/1087/)

Poverty – Who is responsible?

Campaign Against Arms Trade (CAAT) is a UK-based organisation working to end the international arms trade. https://www.caat.org.uk/issues/poverty

Poverty

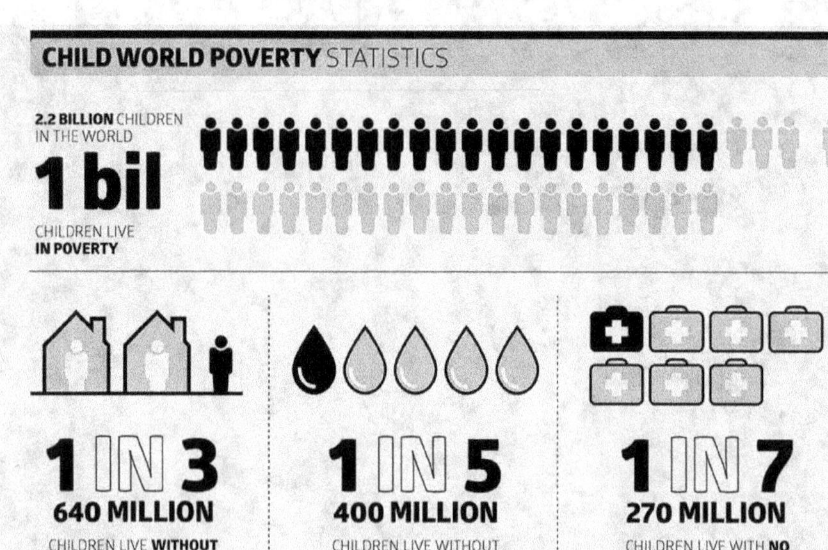

Child World Poverty - http://infographic.ly/portfolio/world-poverty-statistics/poverty-02-2/

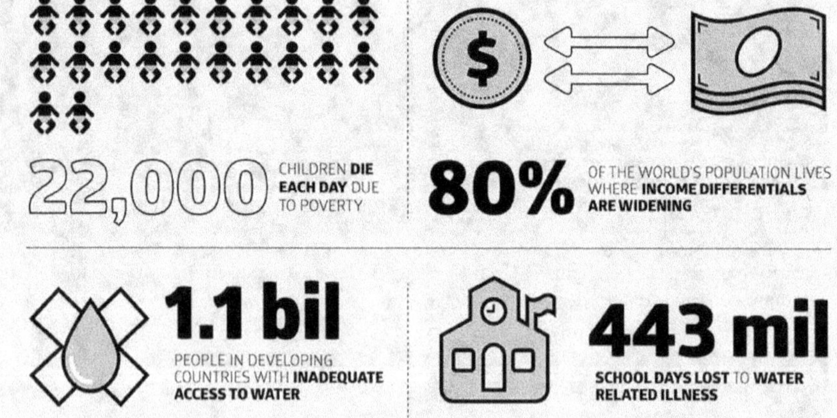

Child World Poverty - http://infographic.ly/portfolio/world-poverty-statistics/poverty-02-2/

6 ARMS CONTROL

The arms trade has had adverse consequences on many nations. The arms trade is immoral and cannot really be justified in any way.. It does not do any good to the human race where millions of people are dying due to wars, poverty, hunger, lack of proper health facilities and environmental damage caused due to many reasons, mainly war.

A Russian-made multiple rocket launcher known as the TOS-1A fires during training at a military camp in Baghdad

The arms trade won't stop unless people will unite themselves and say strong 'NO' for the corruption. People need to realise that this problem must be solved, otherwise it will get only worst. If we will let it happen, we will fight for the countries or country which never cared about any human rights or better future. It never been our fight, it never been our war. People want to live peacefully and arms should be used only to make sure people are safe and secure. Arms must be limited and have positive impact using it to reduce crime level inside and outside the countries. Instead of spending billions governments could use the money to raise economy and help pure countries. If money would be used wisely, we would face brighter future with new technologies, which would help us to invent and explore. Every regular person should care more about the issues which stays in the shadow.

The arms trade has shown us that the developed world supplies more arms than aid to the developing nations, therefore contributing more to conflict. The arms trade has helped many developing governments to build up a mighty military machine to crush internal opposition, to threaten neighbouring countries or to supporters for new territory (as in the case of Iraq's invasion of Kuwait). To that extent it has made the world a more dangerous and bloody place.

Ballistic missile – Arms Control

Moreover, it was revealed how the trade exacerbates conflict, promotes human rights abuses and worsens poverty in developing countries. The most obvious adverse impact of the arms trade on health is loss of life and maiming from the use of weapons in conflicts. Developed countries suffer damage to their health and human services when considerable resources are diverted to military expenditure. However, the relative impact of military expenditures and conflict on developing countries is much higher, and often catastrophic, by depriving a large portion of the population of essential food, shelter, medicine, economic opportunities and education. Furthermore, the physical and psychological damage inflicted specifically on children is harmful – through loss of (or separation from) families, loss of education, destruction of homes, exposure to murder and other violence, sexual abuse, abduction, torture, slavery, and forcible conscription as soldiers.

The money used to buy arms can instead be used to solve the world problems. The amount of money the world spends on arms if used for humanitarian needs would wipe out all diseases/poverty and hunger in many countries in the world. The arms trade is in no doubt but immoral the buying and selling of arms cannot be morally justified.

German Typhoon multi-role combat aircraft

Predator Drone

7 PEACE EDUCATION

The modern world has been prone to an increasing trend in destructive conflicts and wars that have devastated regions across the globe. Since the  First World War, there has been a rapid increase in the development of various methods to kill one another. The massive loss of lives and the human suffering (and also environmental degradation) has continued with an increase in lethality and fervour. Harris (2004) states, "During this past century there has been growth in social concerns about horrific forms of violence, like ecocide, genocide, modern warfare, ethnic hatred, racism, sexual abuse and domestic violence".

Many countries are currently been shaken by violent and intractable conflicts, including Iraq, Syria, Israel, Nigeria, Ukraine and Yemen. The list continues with a number of conflicts across the world that have the potential to cause huge loss of life. The conflict over the disputed territory of Kashmir between India and Pakistan has the potential to escalate to a nuclear level (as both countries possess nuclear weapons).

Arms trade infographic facts - https://blog.amnestyusa.org/africa/is-u-s-trying-to-gut-arms-trade-treaty/

Harris (2004) further mentions that there is, "a corresponding growth in the field of peace education where educators, from early child care to adult, use their professional skills to warn fellow citizens about imminent dangers and advise them about paths to peace".

Culp (2017) argues that, "in the context of violent and intractable conflicts, peace education appears to be an effective instrument to promote peace because it holds the promise to empower future generations to solve many of those problems which present generations have had difficulty resolving". Culp further contends (2017), "Teaching people to interact with each other on peaceful terms is vital for social life of all groups – and even in the absence of any crisis".

Peace Studies does not have a clear agreed definition at this moment. Butt et al., (2011), noted, "Peace is a vague word. For some it means silence, calm and quiet, while other perceive it is an "end to quarrel", no conflict, no war, no violence, or no dispute (Mehmooda, 2006). According to Harris and Synott, Peace Education is a successions of 'teaching encounters' that draw from people:
1)   People's want for peace,
2)   Non-violent alternatives for dealing with conflict
3)   Skills for critical examination of structural measures that produce and legitimize injustice and equality (Harris and Synott, 2004).

Danesh (2006) argues that peace education is an elusive concept and has become more important due to the ever increasing trend of conflicts across the world. Accordingly, current peace education activities have been put under four categories:

Peace education 'mainly as a matter of changing mind-set', peace education 'mainly as a matter of cultivating a set of skills', peace education 'mainly a matter of promoting human rights, and finally, peace education as a 'matter of environmentalism, disarmament, and the promotion of a culture of peace' (Salomon, 2002). Moreover, ten goals for effective peace education had been identified by Harris (2002).

This shows that there has been widespread debate amongst the international community in regards to finding ways of increasing human security via the various processes of peace education.

Ellison (2014), noted the important study by Bush and Satarelli (2000) that had highlighted the "two faces of education and its role in both fuelling and mitigating conflict". In this study a number of examples were provided to show the ways in which education was used to intensify intergroup hostility. Such as the following:

(1) Education used as a weapon in cultural repression (the refusal to allow the Kurdish minority in Turkey to use their language in schools),

(2) Denial of education as a weapon of war (destruction of schools in Mozambique and the forced closure of Palestinian schools by Israel),

(3) Manipulation of textbooks (negative ethnic stereotypes in Rwanda and depiction of Tamils as the historic enemies of the Sinhalese in Sri Lanka).

Ellison (2014) also mentions the numerous studies that have discussed the many ways that the school system might reproduce social and gender inequalities that may be a catalyst for war (Davis, 2004).

Butt et al., (2011), noted, "Peace education is educating all people for peace to satisfy their physical and social needs through individual and group action at the micro (interpersonal) and macro (local, national, and global inter group) levels" (Yousaf et al., 2010). In addition, "The aim of peace education is to draw out, enrich, deepen and place in context students' thinking about the concept of peace" (Bretherton, et al., 2002)

The globalisation of the world and the regular tourism across it has led some to expand on the concept of peace. Ward (2009) has used the term 'peace tourism' in which he describes the term as, "self-initiated travel by an individual citizen to explore a (new) nation and its people using personal resources – time, financial, interpersonal, etc.". He believes that this concept is relevant to, "citizens of nations involved in war, genocide, drug or human trafficking, arms sales or any systematic armed violence against other nations".

Butt et al., (2011), also mentions "that internet, cd-rom, children's books, traditional folk stories, proverbs, art work and artefacts, and language teaching can be used as creative avenues to introduce peace education concepts, skills and attitudes, whether in or out of the school context" (Fountain, Susan, 1999).

The daily news of violent conflicts around the world and the trade in the buying and selling of weapons has increased human misery, poverty and loss of life. Peace education is a way of embedding positive methods to reduce the arms trade and ensure a more peaceful world.

Peace Education needs to become mandatory in all educational institutions and also should be a requirement for all government employees - confirms the positivity in this area and the desire to have this implemented in general education. Butt et al., (2011), further contends, "Peace education is most effective when the skills of peace and conflict resolution are learned actively and are modelled by the school environment in which pupils are taught" (Baldo and Furniss, 1998).

Peace Education can reform individuals positively. Butt et al., (2011), stated "Peace Education is currently considered to be both a philosophy and a process involving skill, including listening, reflection, problem solving, co-operation and conflict resolution. The process involves empowering people with the skills, attitude and knowledge to create a safe world and build a sustainable environment. The philosophy teaches nonviolence, love, compassion, and reverence for all life" (Harris and Morrison, 1988).

There is a high chance that peace education can reduce the arms trade. If more and more people are aware of the alternative methods of resolving conflicts and with individual mind-set changed positively towards a peaceful world. – then the scourge of the global arms trade can be curtailed. The arms trade is the mechanism that fuels the simmering disputes and conflicts across the world.

Devasting firepower of modern weapons

8 CONCLUSION

The arms trade has had adverse consequences on many nations. The arms trade is immoral and cannot really be justified in any way. It does not do any good to the human race where millions of people are dying due to wars, poverty, hunger, lack of proper health facilities and environmental damage caused due to many reasons, mainly war.

Su-35 Fighter Jet

The arms trade won't stop unless people will unite themselves and say strong 'NO' for the corruption. People need to realise that this problem must be solved, otherwise it will get only worst. If we will let it happen, we will fight for the countries or country which never cared about any human rights or better future. It never been our fight, it never been our war. People want to live peacefully and arms should be used only to make sure people are safe and secure. Arms must be limited and have positive impact using it to reduce crime level inside and outside the countries. Instead of spending billions governments could use the money to raise economy and help pure countries. If money would be used wisely, we would face brighter future with new technologies, which would help us to invent and explore. Every regular person should care more about the issues which stays in the shadow.

The arms trade has shown us that the developed world supplies more arms than aid to the developing nations, therefore contributing more to conflict. The arms trade has helped many developing governments to build up a mighty military machine to crush internal opposition, to threaten neighbouring countries or to supporters for new territory (as in the case of Iraq's invasion of Kuwait). To that extent it has made the world a more dangerous and bloody place.

Moreover, it was revealed how the trade exacerbates conflict, promotes human rights abuses and worsens poverty in developing countries. The most obvious adverse impact of the arms trade on health is loss of life and maiming from the use of weapons in conflicts. Developed countries suffer damage to their health and human services when considerable resources are diverted to military expenditure. However, the relative impact of military expenditures and conflict on developing countries is much higher, and often catastrophic, by depriving a large portion of the population of essential food, shelter, medicine, economic opportunities and education. Furthermore, the physical and psychological damage inflicted specifically on children is harmful – through loss of (or separation from) families, loss of education, destruction of homes, exposure to murder and other violence, sexual abuse, abduction, torture, slavery, and forcible conscription as soldiers.

The money used to buy arms can instead be used to solve the world problems. The amount of money the world spends on arms if used for humanitarian needs would wipe out all diseases/poverty and hunger in many countries in the world. The arms trade is in no doubt but immoral the buying and selling of arms cannot be morally justified.

Amnesty international fact - https://www.amnesty.org.uk/

References

Adams, J. (1992). Trading in Death – the Modern Arms Race, Pan Books Ltd.

Amnesty International - https://www.amnesty.org.uk/

Bekerman, Z., & Zembylas, M. (2014). Some reflections on the links between teacher education and peace education: Interrogating the ontology of normative epistemological premises. Teaching and Teacher Education, 41, 52-59. doi:10.1016/j.tate.2014.03.002

Burrows, G. (2002). The No-Nonsense guide to the Arms Trade, New Internationalist Publications Ltd.

Butt, M. N., Iqbal, M., Ud-Din, M. N., Hussain, I., & Muhammad, N. (2011). Infuse concept of peace in curriculum development. Contemporary Issues in Education Research (CIER), 4(2), 27. doi:10.19030/cier.v4i2.4080

Campaign Against Arms Trade (CAAT), Global Poverty, Online - https://www.caat.org.uk/issues/poverty

Cordesman, A.H. (1988). Armed Forces Journal, Western Strategic Interests and the India-Pakistan military balance, Ian Allan Ltd.

Culp, J. (2017). Against all odds: Peace education in times of crisis. Educational Philosophy and Theory, 49(10), 1029-1037. doi:10.1080/00131857.2016.1274954

Danesh, H. B. (2006). Towards an integrative theory of peace education. Journal of Peace Education, 3(1), 55-78. doi:10.1080/17400200500532151

Erickson, J. L. (2015). Dangerous trade: Arms exports, human rights, and international reputation. New York: Columbia University Press.

Freedman, L. (1985). Atlas of Global Strategy, MacMillan London Ltd.

Galtung, J. (1983). Peace education: Learning to hate war, love peace, and to do something about it. International Review of Education / Internationale Zeitschrift Für Erziehungswissenschaft / Revue Internationale De l'Education, 29(3), 281-287. doi:10.1007/BF00597972
Global Issues - http://www.globalissues.org/article/78/small-arms-they-

cause-90-of-civilian-casualties

Gross, Z. (2017). Revisiting peace education: Bridging theory and practice – international and comparative perspectives – introduction. Research in Comparative and International Education, 12(1), 3-8. doi:10.1177/1745499917698290

Harris, I. M. (2004). Peace education theory. Journal of Peace Education, 1(1), 5-20. doi:10.1080/1740020032000178276

Human Rights Watch (HRW) - https://www.hrw.org/news/2009/03/25/israel-white-phosphorus-use-evidence-war-crimes

Imperial War Museum - https://www.iwm.org.uk/history/a-short-history-of-the-falklands-war

Lauritzen, S. M. (2016). Building peace through education in a post-conflict environment: A case study exploring perceptions of best practices. International Journal of Educational Development, 51, 77-83. doi:10.1016/j.ijedudev.2016.09.001

Oxfam - https://www.oxfam.org/en/research/wealth-having-it-all-and-wanting-more

SIPRI Yearbook (2014) – Armaments, Disarmament and International Security, Oxford University Press Inc., New York.

SIPRI - https://www.sipri.org/

Smith Ellison, C. (2014). The role of education in peacebuilding: An analysis of five change theories in sierra leone. Compare: A Journal of Comparative and International Education, 44(2), 186-207. doi:10.1080/03057925.2012.734138
Stavrianakis, A. (2010;2013;). Taking aim at the arms trade: NGOs, global civil society and the world military order. London;New York;: Zed Books.

Stephenson, C. M. (2012). Elise boulding and peace education: Theory, practice, and quaker faith. Journal of Peace Education, 9(2), 115-126. doi:10.1080/17400201.2012.700196

Ward, V. (2009). Conflicts of interest: Plasticity of peace tourism and the 21st century nation. Perspectives on Global Development and Technology,

8(2-3), 414-426. doi:10.1163/156914909X423953

Wessells, M. (2005). Child soldiers, peace education, and postconflict reconstruction for peace. Theory into Practice, 44(4), 363-369. doi:10.1207/s15430421tip4404_10

Wilson, A. (1983). The Disarmer's Handbook of Military technology and organization, Penguin Books.

WHO. (2017, September 15). World hunger again on the rise, driven by conflict and climate change, new UN report says. Retrieved July 19, 2018, from http://www.who.int/news-room/detail/15-09-2017-world-hunger-again-on-the-rise-driven-by-conflict-and-climate-change-new-un-report-says

Images in this book fall under the following categories
(a) public domain (applicable to most official photos released by the military/maufacturers)
(b) free for commercial use
(c) used with explicit permission from the owner (applicable to all images from private websites)
(d) assumed to fall under (a) or (b) (applicable to images in printed media where no image owner is identified)

INDEX

Major changes in East Asia have placed the region near the top of the World's strategic agenda. East Asia has until recently experienced the fastest regional economic growth rate in the world for many years. Economic co-operation has been flourishing and economic interests have become the major reason in reshaping East Asian international relations. However, there have also been changes in the security environment, due to many factors, such as the reduction of US forces in East Asia, the disintegration of the Soviet Union (the decline of the Soviet Union's presence in the region had led to renewed attention to traditional and potential rivalries among the major East Asian powers), and the concern of China's hegemonistic ambitions.

The astronomical rising costs of modern combat has resulted in many countries being deprived of purchasing a modern combat aircraft and this has had an adverse effect on their security. Many nations have tried to undertake cost-effective measures for their defence needs.

Countries can either purchase very expensive modern aircraft or buy older aircraft that can be expensive to operate due to their high maintenance requirements. The Pakistan Air Force had initiated the plan to co-develop an affordable modern multi-role fighter aircraft with China. Chengdu Aircraft Corporation (CAC) in collaboration with Pakistan Aeronautical Complex (PAC, Kamra) have jointly developed the JF-17 Thunder combat aircraft (also known as the FC-1 Xiaolong Fierce Dragon in China).

JF-17 Thunder is a sophisticated light-weight multi-role, all weather, day/night fighter aircraft that is manufactured by Pakistan and China. The JF-17 Thunder has become a very cost-effective aircraft that costs very little compared to other modern aircraft. Many countries have shown an interest and a few have started to make orders. Some have described the JF-17 as the 'Ultimate MiG-21' arguing that the Chinese/Pakistani JF-17 builds on a classic warplane – although it has no resemblance and its level of sophistication is comparable to current advanced fighter aircraft on the market. This very modern and capable aircraft has the potential to become a potent platform that can serve with numerous air forces across the world.

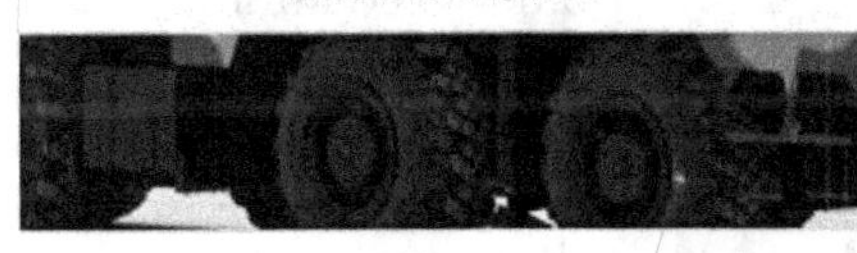

The global security challenges after the post-Cold war period has affected many countries. Pakistan's geography and location present its security planners with serious, almost irresolvable strategic and tactical problems. It borders the nuclear states of India and China, an ambitious Iran, and an unstable Afghanistan, which is perceived as a gateway to its commercial-strategic ambitions in Central Asia.

Pakistan's key security problems are a reflection of its history and domestic circumstances. The overriding concern of Pakistan is its internal and external security. Strategically, Pakistan lacks territorial depth. Its main cities and communication routes are relatively close to the border with India and are susceptible to attack. In addition, the headwaters of Pakistan's rivers and main irrigation systems originate from India. Pakistan's borders with India were also new and mainly unfortified and, in many places, were drawn in ways that made them indefensible. Because the borders were also un-demarcated, there was abundant chance for conflict. Pakistan has particularly been affected with a number of issues.

It has been argued by many that a Fourth generation/Hybrid war has been imposed on Pakistan, in order to break the nation (Balkanization of Pakistan into different parts) with the aim of making it either extremely weak or total destruction as a nation state (so that it is not able to challenge the hegemonistic ambitions of its adversaries).The purpose of this book is to assess the military security problems that Pakistan faces, and focus on its external security matters (military threats from neighbouring countries such as India, balance of power in the region, nuclear and ballistic missile threats, relationship with external powers, the high risk of war and its role on the 'War on Terror'), and its internal security problems (sectarianism, proliferation of small arms, refugees, ethnic violence, drug problem, economic weaknesses), and also its ability to cope with these problems.

MISCALCULATION: RISKS OF
INADVERTENT NUCLEAR WAR

Saghir Iqbal

An impending nuclear holocaust is likely to happen, if the world community does not take action. A conflict that has been simmering for many years is beginning to spiral out of control. Two nuclear powers have an unresolved dispute that has increased tensions in the region.

Both countries are purchasing and developing sophisticated state-of-the-art weapons that could unleash great terror and destruction on the populations of both countries – with also serious global ramifications.

The world's most dangerous flashpoint, has the highest chance of a nuclear war occurring – it is deemed by many to be more serious that the Cuban Missile Crisis and North Korea's nuclear sabre rattling. The dispute needs to be amicably resolved between both nations and confidence building measures need to be implemented.

Pakistan faces a number of threats from internal and external forces — with the aim of weakening the country and an attempt to 'balkanise' Pakistan in to different parts. The Pakistani Chief of Army, General Qamar Javed Bajwa has said that "a hybrid war had been imposed on Pakistan to internally weaken it, but noted that the enemies were failing to divide the country on the basis of ethnicity and other identities".

Furthermore he states, "Our enemies know that they cannot beat us fair and square and have thus subjected us to a cruel, evil and protracted hybrid war. They are trying to weaken our resolve by weakening us from within". Conflicts in Ukraine, Israel and Lebanon (Hizbullah), Syria, Libya, War on Terror in Afghanistan and its impact in Pakistan etc., have resulted in multi-layered efforts to destabilise a functioning state and polarize its society. The centre of gravity is to target population in hybrid warfare. The aim of the adversary is to influence influential policy makers and key decision makers by combining kinetic operations with subversive efforts. The aggressor often resorts to covert actions, to avoid attribution or retribution. At the moment there is no universally accepted definition of hybrid wars — the term is too abstract and is seen by some as using a fancy term to refer to irregular methods to counter conventionally stronger forces.

Accordingly, many say that the new definitions of 4th generation or hybrid wars are really the repackaging of the traditional clash between the armed forces of nation states and the non-state insurgents. This book will be assessing Pakistan's insecurity and the hybrid wars imposed onto it by its adversaries. It will look at a number of issues that Pakistan is facing (military imbalance, economic and political weaknesses, internal and external security threats and the impact of hybrid warfare on Pakistan).

ABOUT THE AUTHOR

Saghir Iqbal is a researcher in International Relations and Security Studies. He is an experienced Intelligence Analyst and has achieved a number of qualifications in this field. He is also a Lecturer in Business Management as well as an Examiner for A Level History and Business. Saghir Iqbal has a subject specialism in the following areas:

International Politics of the Cold War 1945-1991
Conflict Resolution in International Society+
Global and North-South Security Studies
Britain in the World
Disarmament Processes: History and Theory
Nationalism and Ethnicity in Post-Cold War Politics
Middle East: Area in Conflict
European Security
International Politics of the Environment
The United Nations, Peacekeeping and Intervention
Disarmament Processes: Current Problems
Globalisation and the South
International Terrorism
International Politics and Security Studies
Introduction to Peace Studies
Politics of the Global Environment
Regional Security in East Asia
Critical Security studies

Recently released books (2018)

- Dangerous Flashpoints in East Asia: The Military Build-up
- JF-17 Thunder: The Making of a Modern Cost- effective Multi-role Combat Aircraft
- Pakistan's War Machine: An Encyclopedia of its Weapons, Strategy and Military Security
- Miscalculation: Risks of Inadvertent Nuclear War
- Hybrid Warfare and its Impact on Pakistan's Security

Website: www.saghir.co.uk

www.ingramcontent.com/pod-product-compliance
Lightning Source LLC
Chambersburg PA
CBHW070028260726
48658CB00002B/544